# GONELLA

by Eva Bourke and Jay Murphy

> We gave a helping hand to grass —
>   and it turned into corn.
> We gave a helping hand to fire —
>   and it turned into a rocket.
> Hesitatingly,
> cautiously,
> we give a helping hand
> to people,
> to some people...
>
>                    *Miroslav Holub*

SALMON PUBLISHING

Published by Salmon Publishing, Seaport House,
New Docks, Galway, 1985.

Copyright Eva Bourke and Jay Murphy, 1985

Some of these poems have previously appeared in *Poetry Ireland Review*, *The Salmon*, *Cyphers*, *Paris/Atlantic*, *Criterion*, *Writing in the West*, and *Jahrbuch fur Lyrik*.

Photograph for Madman and the Tree: Terri Russell

Typeset by Officina Typographica

## CONTENTS

| | |
|---|---|
| Fish | 2 |
| Child | 5 |
| Garden of Delights | 8 |
| Sphinx Ligustri | 10 |
| Outside The Shelter | 13 |
| Pieta | 16 |
| Frida Kahlo | 18 |
| Heart | 21 |
| Advice On How To Hibernate | 24 |
| Pilgrimage | 26 |
| Defective Mimicry | 28 |
| Dead Swan | 29 |
| Lamentations Of Annie | 32 |
| Zoo | 34 |
| Gonella | 37 |
| The Cricket | 40 |
| Old Men | 43 |
| The Suffering Of The Saints | 44 |
| Sonntag Im Palmencafé | 46 |
| Memento | 50 |
| Two Times Two | 52 |
| Epilogue | 56 |
| A Rat's Tale | 58 |
| Where Has The Draper Gone | 61 |
| After Deportation | 64 |
| Lords Of The Island | 66 |
| The Madman And The Tree | 69 |
| 13 Ways Of Looking At a Rocket | 72 |

Produced with the generous assistance of The Arts Council (An Chomhairle Ealaíon) and Galway Corporation.

Published by Salmon Publishing

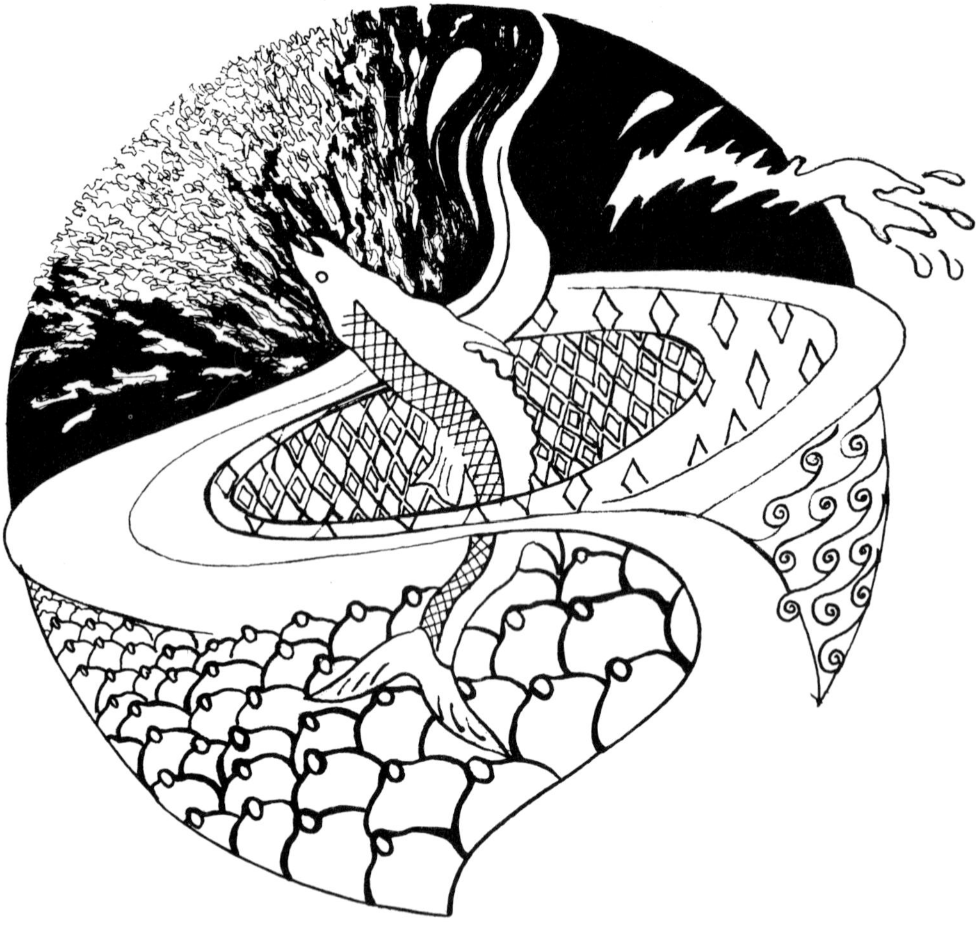

# THE FISH

And what, if it had been a fish
in the beginning,
not the word, or the power, or the deed.
A fish,
sky-blue,
or pre-cardinal red,
or sienna brown,
(before Troy was ever heard of).
A fish in the sky with diamonds
and sapphires.
A fish whose fins
brush the equator.
A fish full of milky tits
suckling the stars.
(There would never have been a thing
like Ganymede,
half ice and half cosmic dust,
circling around a barren planet.)
There would have been streams
and tropical seas
at a very habitable temperature.
The fish would have seen to this,
for even god-fish want to survive.

There would have been no need
for anyone's son's sacrifice,
no need for supplication and betrayal
in any particular olive grove,
none for the gathering of blood
in chalice or grail,
none for holy wars,
nor genocide.
Can you imagine
fish roe begetting a field
of steely warriors.
Never.
No baby fish would thrive
in the type of soil
that threw up armies.

We would have been lanterns
of finely beaten metal.
Drifting lights,
children of wave and alga,
children's children of the salts,
constellations in a glass world
of aquamarine and indigo,
with the spice of seaweed and ocean foliage
in our mouths,
yellow-ringed, with fragile gills,
moving opalescent fins
as showers of sparks
through sea-caves,
fireworks descending on cushions
of chrysoprase
in coral woods.

Why did we not choose the fish
when we were still able to?
Why did we love our own image so,
armoured in steel,
at best full of misery,
too heavy to float,
always busy
sowing dragon teeth.
The chance was gone
at the flick of a tail fin.

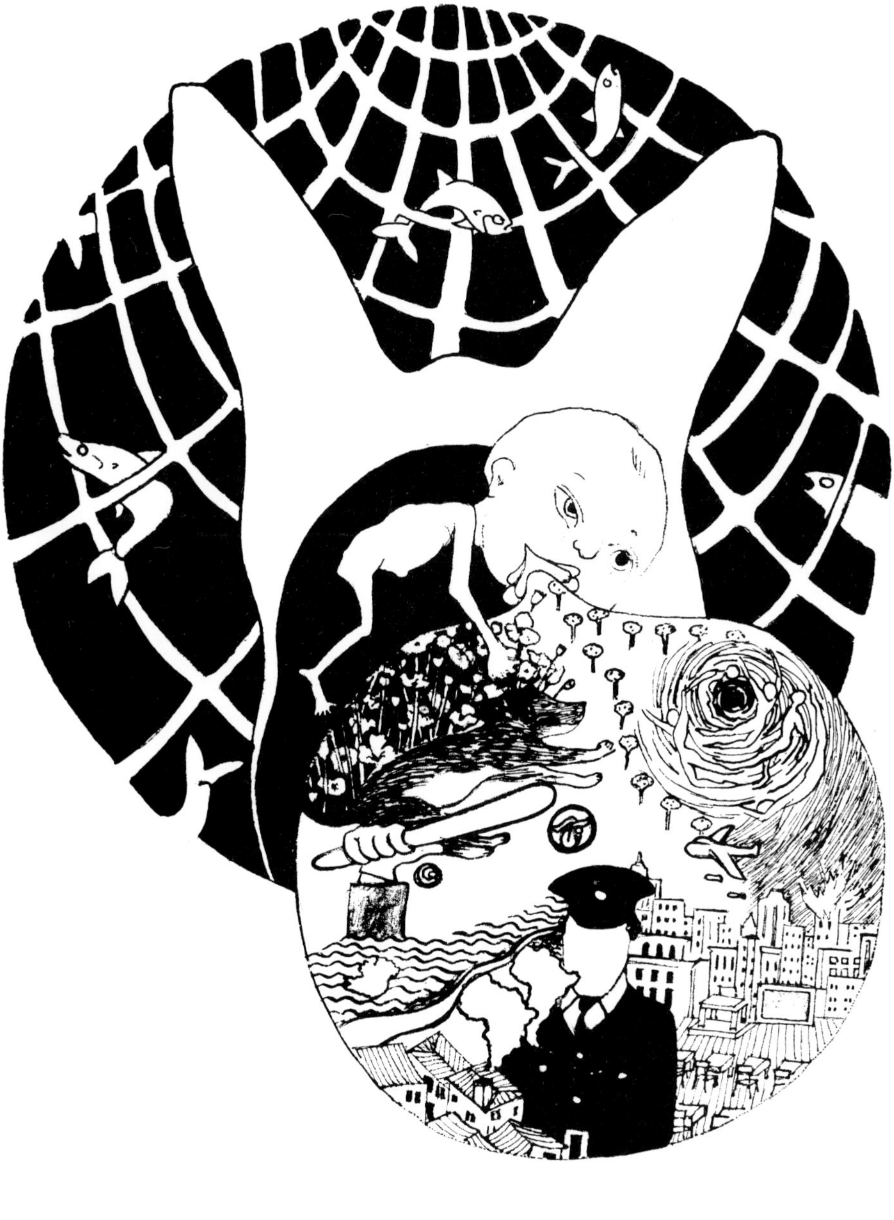

# CHILD

With your head of amber
and your slumbering teeth,
I have taken you out of me
like a loaf of bread.

Now the oven is cold
and robbed of its aroma.
You lie on me,
a new cake,
more unheeding than a swallow
that makes love in flight,
more wilful than a nestling cuckoo.

You tremble on my body,
a string just plucked,
a dancer become tired,
the point of an arrow.

Your mouth surrounds me
with the sucking arms
of the tender young cuttle-fish.
You suck from me houses,
islands, workshops, continents,
sea-roads, policemen, ball games,
small dogs, orange-trees, metropolises,
schoolrooms, contortionists,
wars, roundabouts and death,
a meadow where poppies
climb higher than the boughs of trees.

My flower full of blood.
My net full of small fish,
with your cobweb fingers,
with your face
made of bread and milk,
of age-old tidings
and hunger,
your mouth that wants to say wind and salt,
the cadence of your voice
that reaches us late
like the light of a nova,
with your shoulders of sheep's wool,
the secret in your clenched fists,
your feet with nails of glass
and mother-of-pearl,
your knees of gravel
and your body of translucent foam.

I see your heart beating:
two weights the eyes,
two weights the hands,
two weights the feet,
my heart your pendulum.

## THE GARDEN OF DELIGHTS

We entertain grave doubts
as to whether he was really there;
the more so since there is
no reliable proof
that he existed at all.

The rumour
that he had strolled into our garden
in the company of his friend
the two-legged dog
whose ears reach down below his waist,
presenting a serious threat
to our hard-won social structures,
was spread around by the priests
the claw-footed bats,

and later confirmed
by the undauntable porcupine
who claims to have espied
from her position
behind the strawberry bushes
something white and dappled
with the longest neck
she had ever seen –
and although an expert in fabulous creatures,
she just couldn't take her eyes off it.

Our council has decided therefore
to hand the matter over
to the Museum of Natural Wonders
where we are proud to have on show,
among other exhibits,
the shell of a griffin's egg,
several human craniums,
part of the smile of a sphinx

plus now this light shadow
as presented in the portrait:
with tall neck, spotted skin,
double horns (very pointed)
and cleft hoofs;

we maintain, however,
and do not fail to point out:
an eye-witness acount
of precisely nothing.

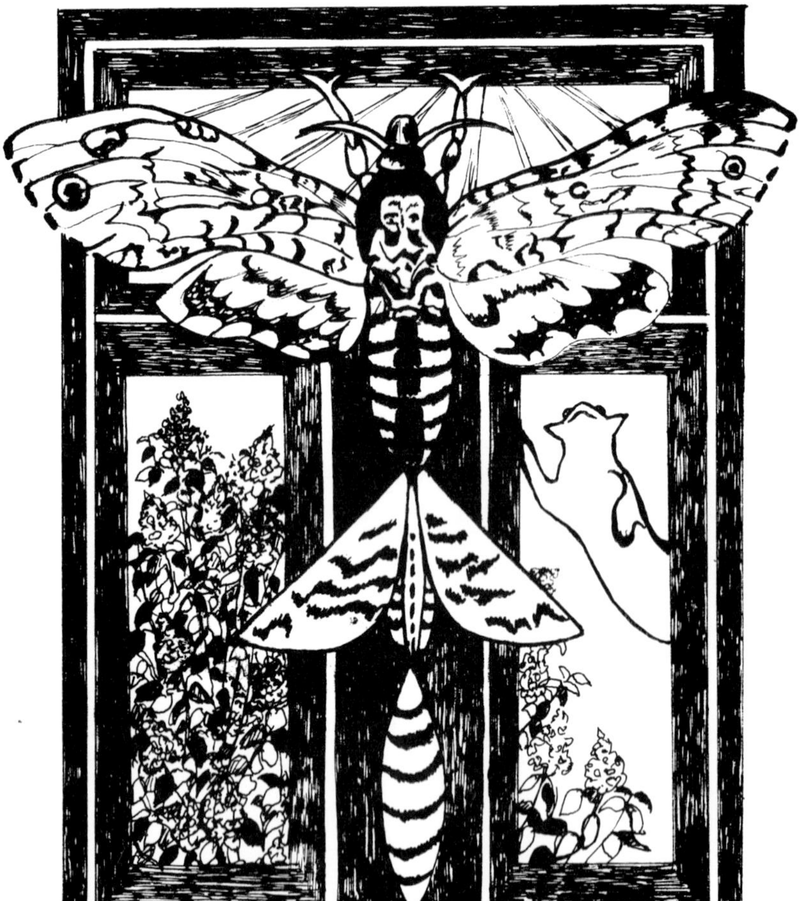

## SPHINX LIGUSTRI

They achieve complete metamorphosis
buried underground,
in spineless claustrophobia,
at the mercy of hormonal plans
like ourselves.
Lime-grey chrysalides of an imago
controlled by nectar smells,
for instance flowering lilac;
'on the wing at dusk
from May to June'
intoxicated by the moon.

How advanced they are.
The tricks they know,
whole sleeves full of them,
colour changes,
optical illusions,
in conspiracy with light
for camouflage
or sexual lure.

On the needles of moth-hunters,
relics behind glass:
Sphinx, Death Head,
Eyed Hawk, Emperor.
Their tiger bodies' plush
faded and dusty,
warning signals
powdered on their wings
spread to open
dark-pupilled eyes
of a cat face,
or wearing a human skull
like a jewel on their thorax.

They are perfect survivors,
programmed to continue ahead of us.
Their head start grows
as their numbers decline.

Night-fliers,
tapping on bright windows,
circling from sweetness
to death
like us.
Below leafy roofs,
when up-wind comes
and morning twilight we meet
as old friends,
exchange a silent code
of trust or caution:

Be vigilant,
don't shun the light.

## OUTSIDE THE SHELTER

The shelter closes its door
painted in brown oil
for the day.

It faces a ruin
of four granite storeys.
There is a brass door-knob
but no knocker.

For the woman outside the shelter
there is a narrow sill
and always the pavement,
while she strings up
beads, or braids
a green and black head-band.

The Atlantic is round the corner
in a basin
below the dust of coal-boats
and fertilizer,
the pier soft to the foot
with mesh of green and orange netting.
And only up the road

the three dark semi-circles
of the bridge over the river's
rise and ebb.
Triads of small waterfalls
pass on fish and sticks
and the grey foam of pollution.
On fine breezy days jobless men
play cards on grass embankments.
Boys lean on bridge walls
staring at the point where a slim
hooked copperfish went under.

The woman has crossed the bridge
many times without seeing the shoals
of young mullet
turn belly-up
and blink signals
and drift into the bay,
so many strips of tin-foil.

She talks to a branch
of wilted leaves in her hand:
'Let him see if he gets
away with it' –
the tape on her ribs,
the knocked-out teeth,
the strangle mark.

    \*   \*   \*

She hits the tight goat skin
of a tambourine,
kicks out barefooted
an Allegria's staccato steps
gathering the wool folds
in her black and brown plaid skirt.

On the tables behind her
bell shapes of wine glasses,
peelings of a pomegranate's
parchment wrap,
a slice of melon light
and vinegared fish,
pencil-thin
on a plate.

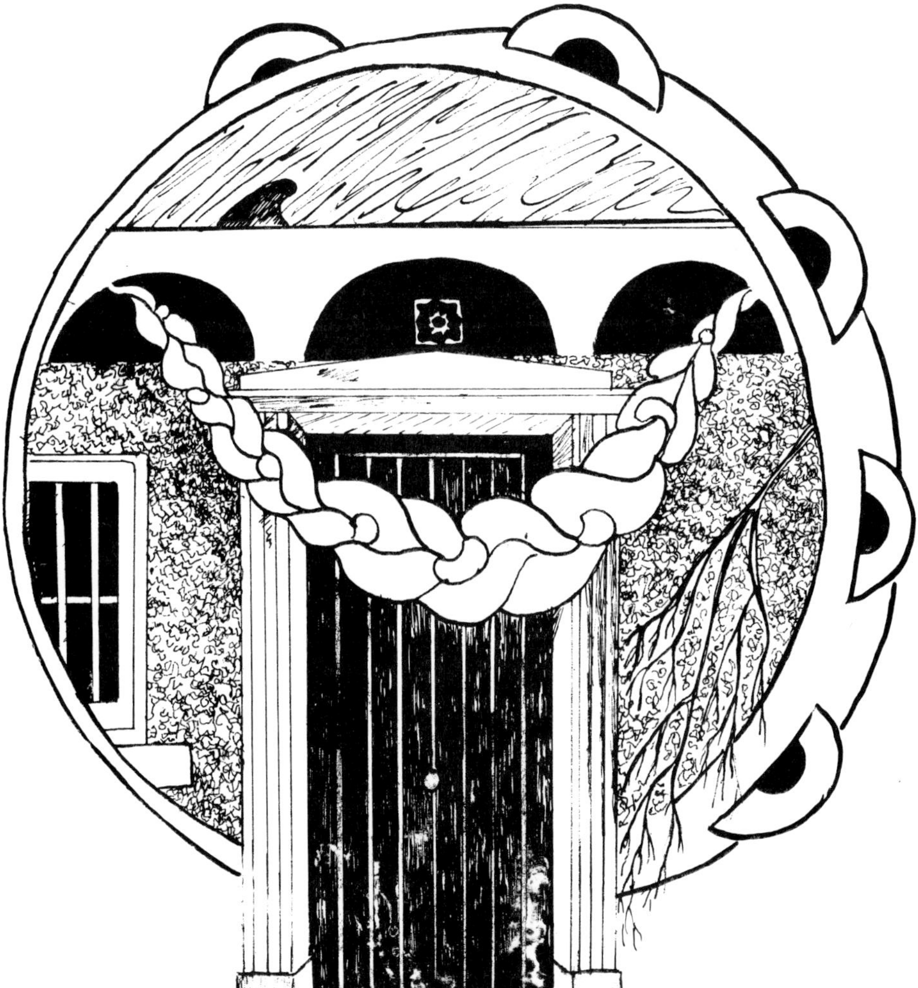

## PIETA

The bucket's mouth is open.
It could swallow the world.
The light crawls into it
through a tracery of tamarind branches.

They have drowned my child.
My husband, my father, my brother
talk to me of economics.
It confuses me.
Pain and hunger is what I know.
I have been well coached in this.
Across the ocean, fat bakers
are setting higher prices
for bread. I see their white fingers
working the till.
My daughter must die, theirs can live.

The helpers are still here
and their helpers.
My mother, my grandmother,
my friendly neighbour.

They whisper and wrap her like a sweet
in pale cotton. I watched
their hands in the bucket,
a dark aquarium, ducking her till she bobbed,
head down, air bubbles breaking the surface.

Her skull of gristle dangles
in its skin bag.
What a picture it makes
with its marbled markings of acid-blue veins.
An early clematis choked by frost,
her mouth forever knotted on a scream,
her tiny lungs crumpling
like two pink balloons.

So tired of life so quick?
Here are my loom, my bundles
of see-through material, my jars of dye
a blur of colours in the corner.

Here is my earthenware dish of scented cream,
my box of silver rings and anklets.
I have kept all this for you.
I say your name every time I breathe.

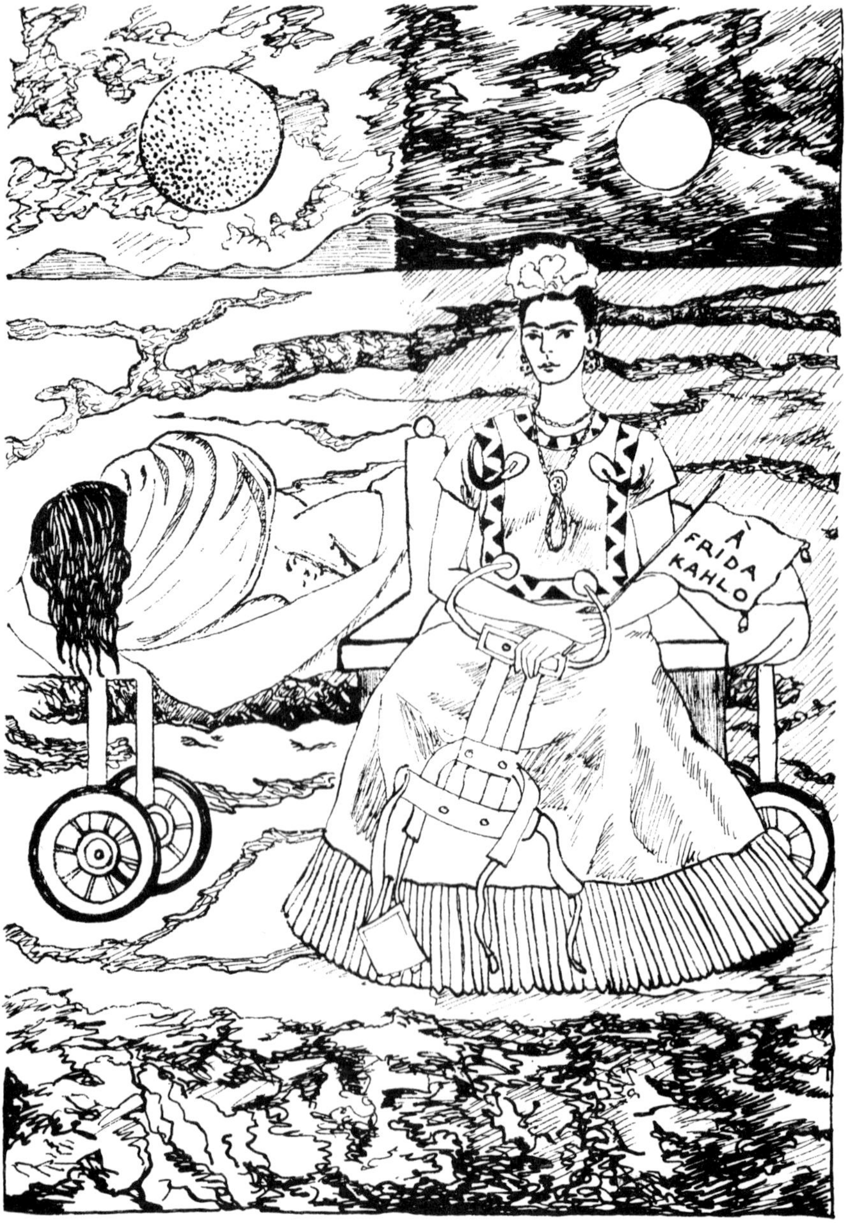

À
FRIDA
KAHLO

# FRIDA KAHLO

*Arbol de la esperanza.*
*Mantente firme.*

Small game,
little daughter,
which huntsman crowned
your light-grey flanks,
your tender breast with nine arrows?
Nine blood-red geraniums blossom
on your antelope's body.
How will your small black hooves
support the weight of your wounds
through this neverland of barren trees
and forked lightning?

Frida,
little sister,
which surgeon broke into you,
smashed the straight column
of your spine and put it back together,
like a badly fitting jigsaw?
Corsetted into straps and bandages,
your torn body barely keeps
from falling apart.
Who tacked the skin back
to your bones, your face,
driving out the tears?

Frida,
little mother,
sorrowful mother of the bleeding back.
When the sun is out,
you are bound to the surgeon's table.
I see your black mane hanging over its end.

The nurses swaddle you in shimmering gauze,
their wounded baby.
The cruel sun makes you wear
your thousand screams openly,
a wreath of steel-nails.
White in surgical cotton,
lined by stitches of hibiscus-red,
you are the afterbirth of violence.

But the moon unwinds you.
She puts you on her throne.
It is made from the tree of hope.
Her pale kindness unfastens your belts,
opens your zips and rivets.
In mooncountry you are the supreme
ruler of colour.
In your blue house every torment
turns into a flower,
a carved necklace of bones
and shells,
a small dark-eyed monkey.
There will be no more suffering.
You stay firm.

## THE HEART

Great-grandmother evolution
came along
and reclaimed her temporary gifts:
pine-cone scale skin
of the crocodile fish,
the bird snake's sharp-toothed beak,
prehensile foot-fingers
with 38 joints each,
the flying ape's steering tail
and very long arms.

Now we walk on soles,
yet there is a memory
of more than five toes.
We walk upright
and sleep lying,
weighed down by our outsize brains,
cradled by the horizon.

But the big change came
with the heart:
we emerged from the water,
flew into the air,
settled on tree branches
and the heart began –
for reasons known only to itself –
its long career
as an anatomical metaphor,
more worn out now
than an old schoolbag.
Who would care for it still,
spruce it up for parties,
address it publicly,
make it a present of one's own?
Schweig stille mein Herze.

It also doesn't worry Hydra,
the tiny fresh-water
polyp,
which sways its star wreath
of alga-coloured tentacles
with the current.
And Medusa,
caressing the salty hollow
of a wave's knee,
a bell-shape of purple-stained
inkblot beauty,
but quite without heart,
uncurls and curls arms
lined with burning cells
tightly like a fist
around nothing,
a hollow centre,
knowing no more
than light and gravity.

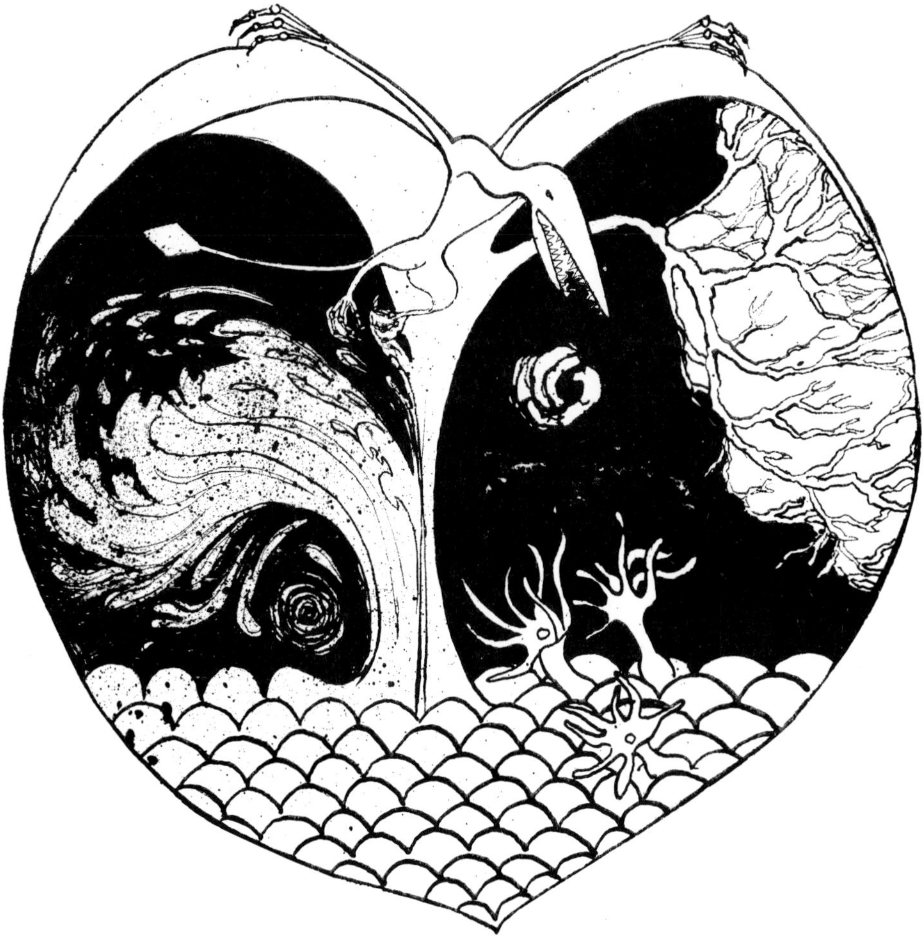

## ADVICE ON HOW TO HIBERNATE

You should wear the sheep pelt
over a sheep skin,
it is rough.

Assign to the tamed wolf
his place by the fire.

When sleeping, face the same way
as your partner.

Think highly of dreams,
less of metaphors
and nothing at all of news.

Don't read papers, letters or telegrams
and keep your fingers
away from birds' entrails.

Hold a close watch instead
on increasing signs of seasonal changes,
inaccuracies
and fog banks.

Whatever you do, don't stir up
the rats' nests by the sea,
but have a few stones ready
for straying dogs.

Kiss the bear-hunter
and ignore the neighbour's evil eye.

Walk the prescribed number of steps
with funeral processions,
cross yourself outside churches
and follow the rituals.

Never cause offence.
That way you might
get through the next winter
without serious trouble.

## PILGRIMAGE

The heavens pour out their bowl,
at pilgrimages they still
have a role to play,

much tender blue and snow how white,
a specifically Bavarian light.
Frosty trees transubstantiate

into dripping candles,
fences march in procession
around snowed-in cabbage patches,

twin shadows of silage towers
lie low on the snow blanket.
Cross-roads are marked by crucifixes.

Autobahn exit DACHAU,
white and blue notices document
a final solution.

The country road to Our Lady of the Peartree
is tarred with ice and instantly
the snow turns red,

the soil is drenched with blood.
The Swedes raged here once,
we are told by the church guide.

A pieta, mutilated by the soldiery,
thrown into a pond,
later on fished out and hidden

in a hollow peartree, caused
the first miraculous cure in 1652
and is still active.

Votive paintings dated up to today
tell of wonderful deliverances
from floods, falling trees,

lightning, polio, twisted ankles, etc.
The merciful image remained merciless
towards the cruel death of millions

through hunger, torture and the gas chamber,
having all its hands full
with the local population.

The guide book tells us how the church
with its three arched cupola roofs
presents a most decorative picture.

The stucco work rates among the richest
ever created by southern German
craftsmen, famous for their tricks

with light and space.
Nearby the watch towers and ovens
surrounded by the gloriole

of barbed wire,
another example of Bavarian
architecture.

Mary is concentrating
on her dead son,
on whirly silver clouds

float unsympathetic little angels.
Twelve apostles
gaze ecstatically down

from the light dome,
and the one
whom we encounter outside the church

in gold loin cloth
and crown of thorns, hangs
quietly with downcast eyelids.

# DEFECTIVE MIMICRY

That my head has neither
facetted eyes
nor antennae
is regrettable.
That my body is not armoured
with chitin plating
must have been an oversight.
That I can't sleep peacefully
like a dog,
trusting in my fangs
and my fine sense of smell,
troubles me.

I have to face the facts:
My organism knows no camouflage.
It can't adapt.
I don't disappear
in the foliage of trees
as veined leaf
among veined leaves.
I know too little about the tactics
of the Ichneumon fly
to imitate it.
And were I to rest
on the bark of an old olive-tree
everyone would see me.

Imperfect, badly equipped,
visible at all times,
I make the best
of what I have:
I clench my fists
in the light of day.

## DEAD SWAN

Headless, neckless, keeled-over
in the still water of the canal.
'He's been there for over
three days',
the dead swan,
his bow
of a stranded ship
between reed and rush.

Swan-white waterlily,
who will pluck it?

'No-one cares about him
until he begins to stink',
a reasonable voice
beside me at the parapet.

Which bridge-walker
heard his death-song?
Who saw how
his wings opened
at the final dance,
petals of a big feathered blossom?

Swallows drove the mosquitoes away.
Bats picked parasites
from his down.
Bluebottles decked him out
with lapis lazuli and beryl.
Pike and rat with little ones
swiftly salvaged the foul treasure.

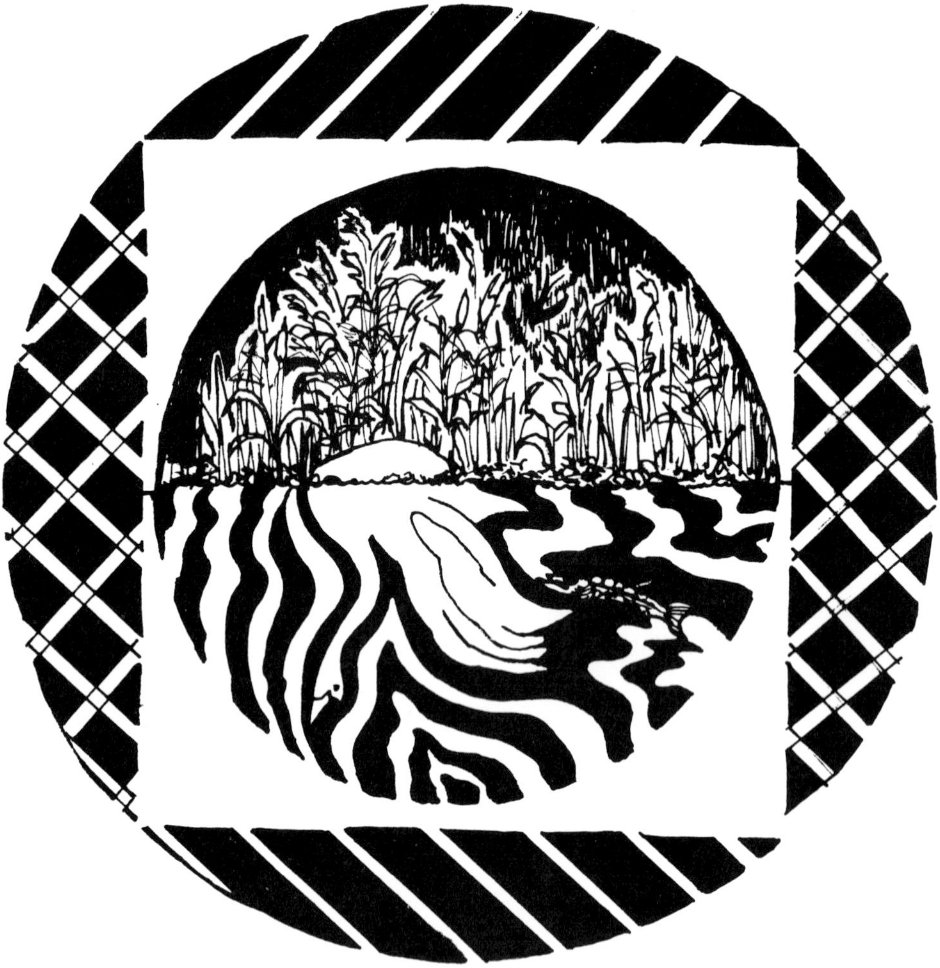

A dead swan
within city limits
outside all jurisdiction.

Unwanted fly-in,
non-resident,
Cygnus Cygnus,
beautiful dead white singer.

# THE LAMENTATIONS OF ANNIE

I put up my claim
outside the bakery in High Street.
Here I tap the copper mine
in passing ladies' pockets.
My working hours are well over forty,
yet I have no beggars' union
to contend my rights.
Should I picket my employer man,
my Joseph in black and red checked cap?
I am Madonna of the cardboard box,
of the broken back at 35.

Cross my palm with silver,
mistress of the bungalow,
always in a hurry from shop to shop
while your husband
is scraping the pavement with nervous shoes.
I'll say ten Hail Marys for you.
Your life rises and swells,
a well-baked loaf,
mine is a piece of stale bread
crunching between my teeth.

I was mothered by misery.
Misery is my legacy
to my thirteen children.
Stuffed away they are in a plastic tent,
a rubbish bag by the roadside,
their bowels coughing up blood
and slime.
Their year is one hard season
of winter nights.
Earth turned her cold back
on them, moon her dark side.

The others don't like my smell.
I am an onion to bring tears
to their eyes.
Below my seven layers
of charitable rags
my heart murmurs and screams,
turning my lips blue:
Why do their doctors not heal us,
their builders not house us,
their teachers not teach us?

Their god is good.
A milkwhite dove.
Mine is a dark and vicious bird.
He took my youngest child on the market place
and flung it under the wheels of a truck
that knocked me down
with an angry red face.
Waking up in hospital
I saw the Bleeding Heart by my bedside
bending over me.
I turned away.
That day the Pope danced his holy dance
in a carpeted park,
spreading his arms wide.
Not wide enough for me,
not wide enough for my child.

## ZOO

It is as if
we had never
seen red before.

This red
brooks no competition.

What is red,
asks the blind man.
How is one to tell him?
(Blood he can only taste):
broken rays
thrown about
in a freezing universe.

China's rising sun,
the devil's silk cloak,
a bowl of strawberries.

The birds inside
the mesh dome of the aviary,
red from beak to claw,
nesting on leafless branches
of artificial trees, are

so red that imperial purple,
vermilion and shocking pink
leave in a hurry
with bowing and scraping.

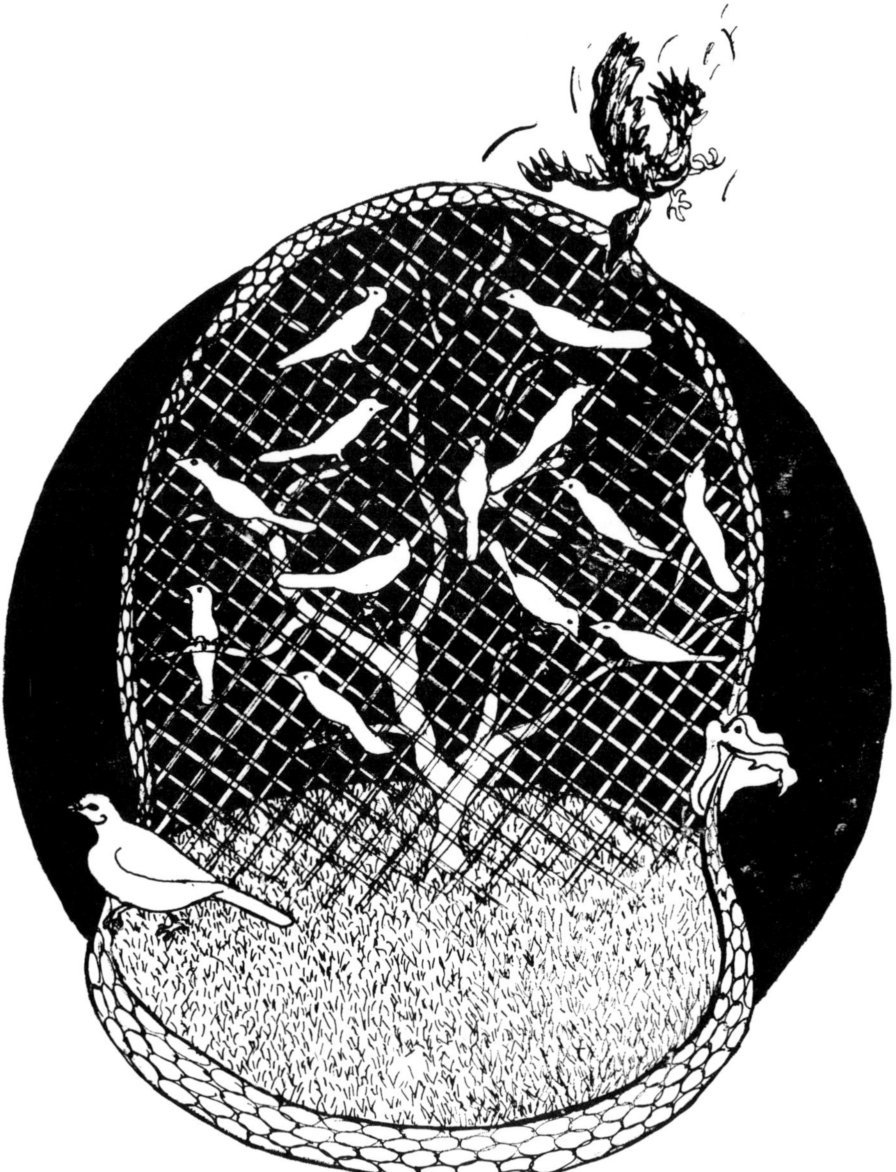

The crows nose-dive
with envious longing
towards so much colour,
it's a joke
how they wriggle
in the net.

Fat blue crowned pigeons
wobble past in the grass
like country buses
cooing ceremoniously
and turning up their feather collars
with studied disdain.

All invention is surpassed
by what's real.

We even begin
to believe in the red death bite
of the venomously green
venomous grass snake.

# GONELLA

Gonella isn't funny anymore.
The jester of the Ferrarese court
refuses to do his act.

Tonight the court wants to be
amused by Gonella.
Old Blear-eye, show us your misery
to make us howl.

Look at Gonella
glowering in his corner,
his fists under his arms.

Gonella has been seen
by our spies.
He has been seen in dark alleys
whispering to young men
from the mountains
who carry halberds.

Gonella, know your place, you cretin.
We, the Count of Ferrara,
want to laugh at your crooked moon-face
tonight. No use hiding
your black tooth-stump behind
that tight-lipped grin.
We can boil you in oil –
remember the last time, Gonella?

You got the sun
on your brain, scum.
We have nine-tailed whips.
Gonella wants to feel them
on his rebellious hump,
that might make us laugh.

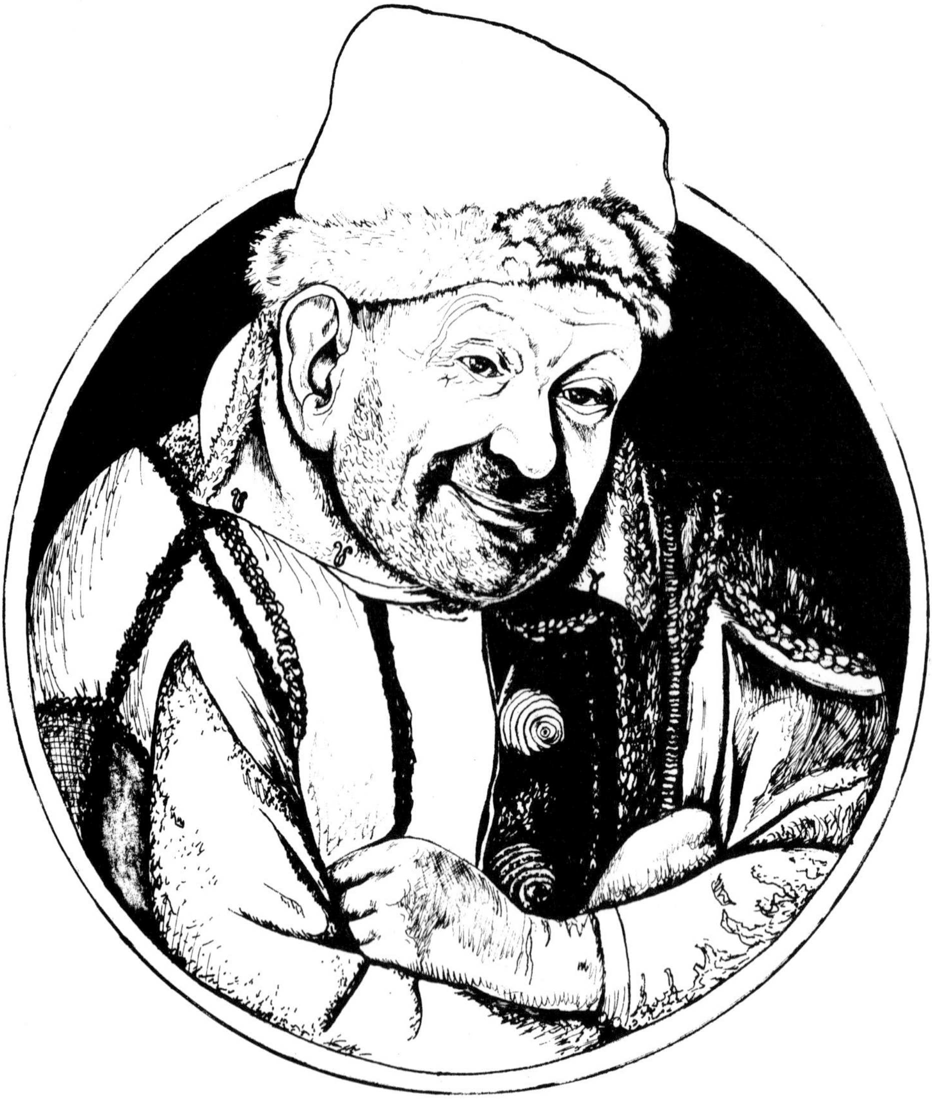

Half-wit in your fool's cap
trimmed with mangy fox tail.
To think what you think you know
about the sun
would give a fool
thoughts beyond his station.

We are your lord,
as it is written into the sky
by God's own finger.

Take your fists from under your arms,
Gonella, or we'll have to break them
open with our screws.

We heard all about you
consorting with the jugglers
and buffoons in the piazza,
who sing the earth down
from high heaven.
Ignorance would do them better.
People have been burned at the stake
for less.

Gonella, it's blasphemy to believe
we live on a lump of stone
rolling around a star
into ever-widening space.

We, your master, and the Holy Church
have given you
your red and yellow dress
with buttons as big
as eggs from Lombardy,
we are robed in purple, silver and ermine.

You think what we tell you.
We rule,
you act the fool or die.

# THE CRICKET

The cricket says: always the same.
With its back legs
it plays:
always the same tune.

I search the sky:
Orion is no longer
where he was before.

Cricket, you deceive yourself.
You live in the dead eye
of the hurricane.

With your rasp-rasp
you neither pierce
the fruit-skin of things,
nor cut off
the wind's breath.

Everything comes again,
grates the cricket.
Its grating
saws through my ear nerve.

Repeating yourself
doesn't make you an oracle,
let me tell you.

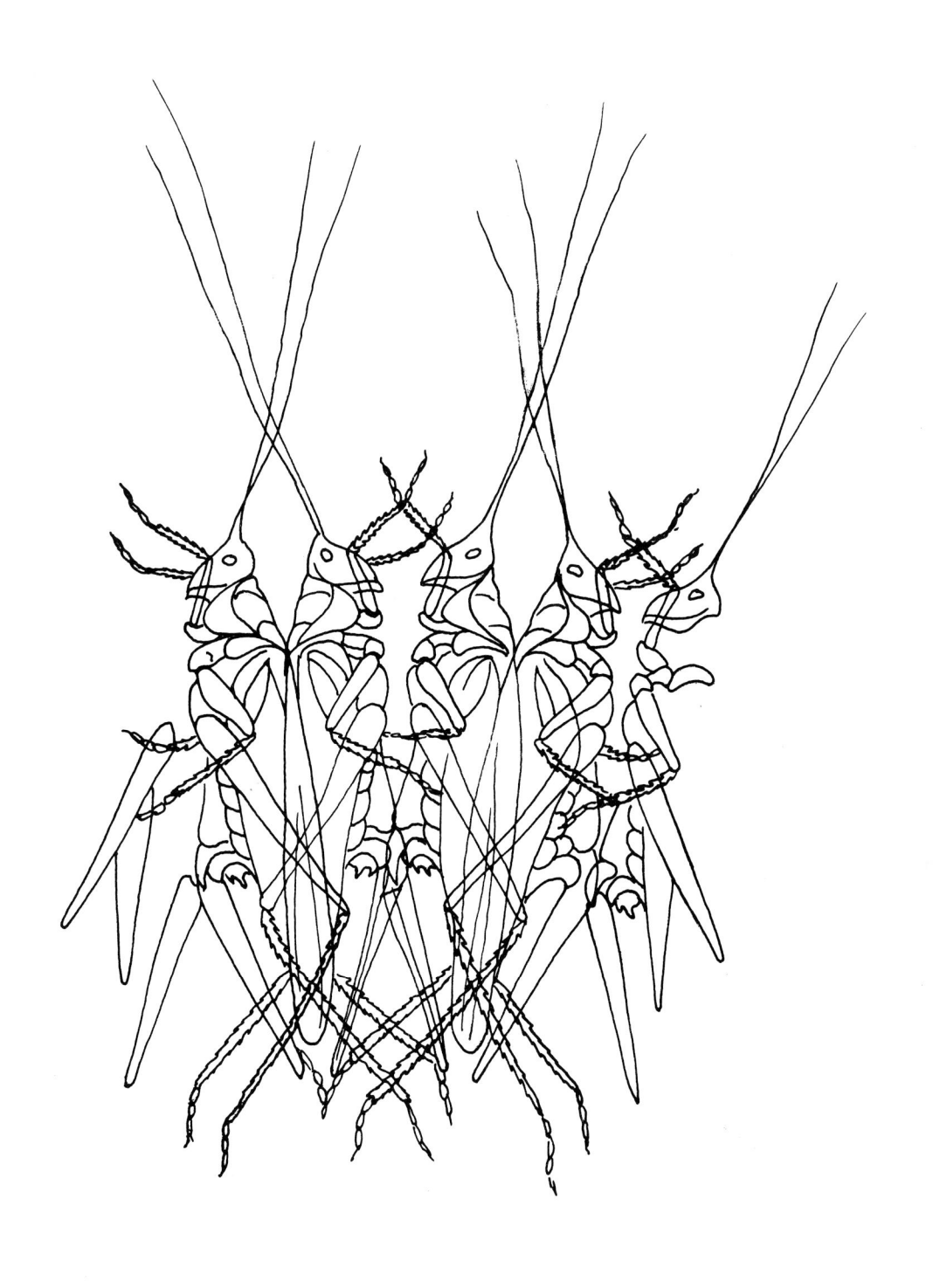

I didn't call for you, cricket.
Nothing comes again.
We turn and twist upwards,
sometimes with pain.

Why don't you leave the bark
and the meadow,
and try your humdrum rhetorics
elsewhere,
below the blackish trees
by the lake, for instance.

Debate with the frogs
at swamp level.

When you have grasped
water and muck,
come back, cricket.

## OLD MEN

More crooked than their houses
they stand in half-open doors,
a peace treaty with life
signed and in their pockets.

The last kernel
of their time –
a fragrant fruit of many segments –
is lying ready
to be spat forth
in their cheek's cave.

Unlike mussels
which open up to die,
they peer through narrowing gaps
between their lid shells
at the low sun.

# THE SUFFERING OF THE SAINTS

You pay only three Marks
admission –

less if you are a child,
soldier or pensioner –

into rooms that are lined
with subdued velvet.

But the tones in the paintings are shrill:
there is hammered gold,
here scorched yellow,
throttled blue,
piercing green.

The torturer on the left
with his rusty brown boots
laced up the back –
he is just about to put
more wood on the pyre –
has been staged
with loving care,
his hook-nosed profile
red from the heat.

The saints are extinct,
as are the painters of their agony,
but not the tormentors:
they work,
now more than ever,
with the sullen absorption
of their Gothic colleagues.

We see how
the saint hovers
slightly above the glowing grid
with no signs of burning
on his white body,
a case, apparently,
of patronage from above.

His head lies
on a golden disc.

On the next altar piece
he will don episcopal brocade
and perform miracles.

Relieved
and noiseless,
we can steal out
over the glossy parquet
past the drowsing custodian.

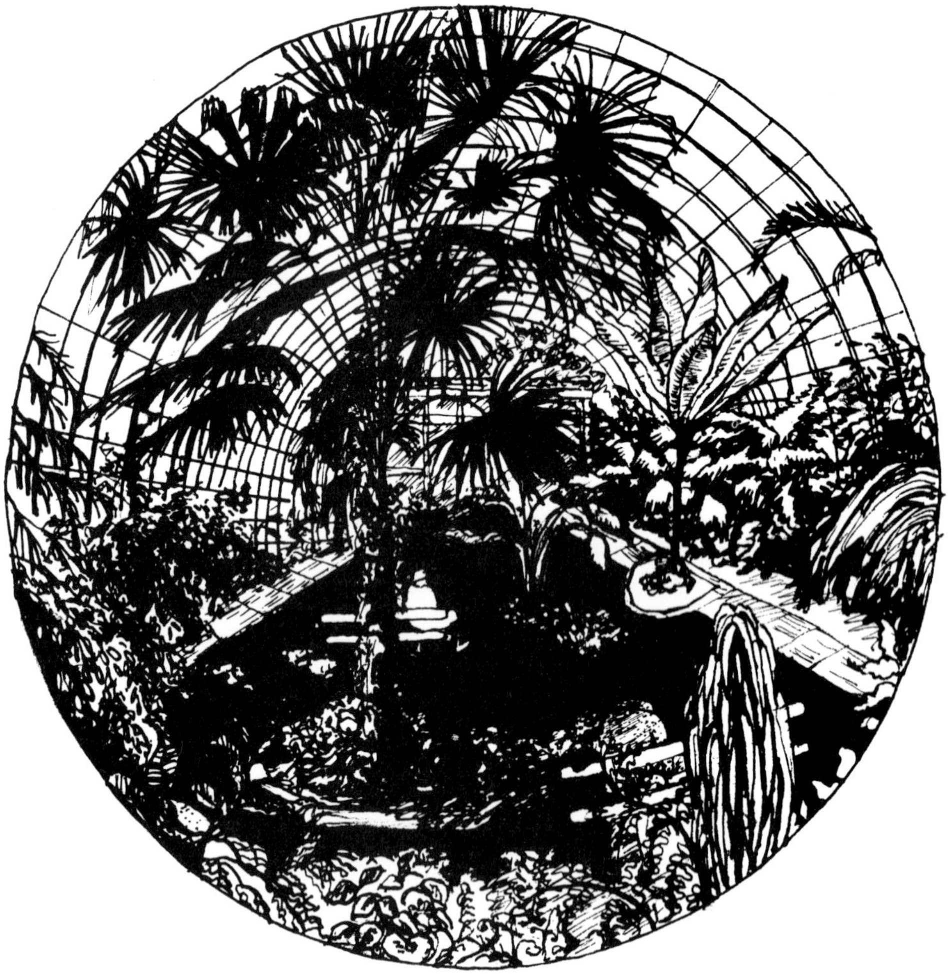

## SONNTAG IM PALMENCAFÉ

I
It's late October.
The castle grounds
in the hermetic pruned neatness
of French gardens admit
Sunday families
come to see how kings live.
They troop, obeying pebbled walk
and well-clipped yew hedge
past Judith and her sword of stone,
Venus' S-curved coyness,
tree-nymphs
and scale-covered water-gods,
around to the lake,
water-bird territory now,
where monarchs used to have their flings
in the silver and blue folly,
easily reached by a hundred strokes
of a duck's webbed foot.

II
In the snake house
children – spellbound by death –
press their faces against a cage
where the shake-rattle-and-roll
dance between the snake
and a tiny white mouse
has begun,
then return to cakes

and hot chocolate,
heated as if rubbed up
the wrong way,
fidgeting in the parental net
of authority and concern
below the transparent roof
of the café
which is supported by the slim-stemmed foliage
of tall palm trees.

III
Come a few steps further
where the door opens
on the green stillness of a glass dome,
but what goings-on inside,
sparked off
by the revolving sprinkler,
a few sun rays
and a constant temperature of 28 degrees:
unfolding of infant leaf,
swaying of stems,
vine curling and unrolling of fern,
twining of choking creeper,
splitting of soil,
probing of root tip.
Small paths circle around
a flowering hibiscus –
it's late October –
a single banana tree screens
with fan-tail leaves
the old women beneath it on the benches.
Aerial roots hurry down to them.
Multitudes of little purple blossoms
strung-up on green threads
trail their hair,
brush their cheeks.
This is a sheltering place for the old,
the left-over.

It is quiet here
except for plant language.
It is warm in the toxic warmth
of many plant bodies together.

They have planted their feet on the ground.
One here, one there.
No leg-pull of vanity
could make them cross their knees again.
They have a slow puncture
in their hearts.
They take root.

# MEMENTO

In my pockets you will find particulars. Age,
last address – dark and cold from neglect
after the sister's death – my pension book,
a memorandum of want, of too little for light,
heat and food.
There are also the name and address of my last
relation in the mental home near Philadelphia.
Too far gone to remember me, shadowy on a wooden
bench of the day room, she shifts feet back
and forth in her institution slippers.
I am leaving all that behind. My life has gone
sour on me like a rotten fruit.
When you read this, brothers and sisters, I am on my way
to you. Let the sea do its job, its machinery
of knives and shears, teeth and pincers cut me,
grind me and pass me through mouths of shark
and eel, shrimp and slug, and mingling with the waves
I rise above them with the mist.
From the shores of Connemara in the clouds I cross
Istanbul at twelve on a blue day, Manila on a rainy
morning. I am headed for you
wherever you are in prison camp, stadium, township,
gulag or on death row, watch for me, a signal,
blades of grass on the window of your freezing cell,
a cooling shower in the fire-edged night
of El Salvador.
I drum on corrugated tin roofs of East Cape,
on the dumpdwellers' cardboard shacks at Rio,

wherever huddled masses are yearning to breathe free,
drumming the rhythm of liberty and rebellion,
I am at the feet of a thousand homeless children,
I cleanse the wounds of those who were tortured,
water-carts and buckets carry me to you
on the margin of glowing deserts made fertile and green,
in the coffee plantations of Nicaragua, planted
with defiance and hope. I am a drink in your cup,
a glistening spray on the whale's back,
I flow past you in the stream and lifting your eyes
to the mountains you will see me bending over them
in the rainbow.

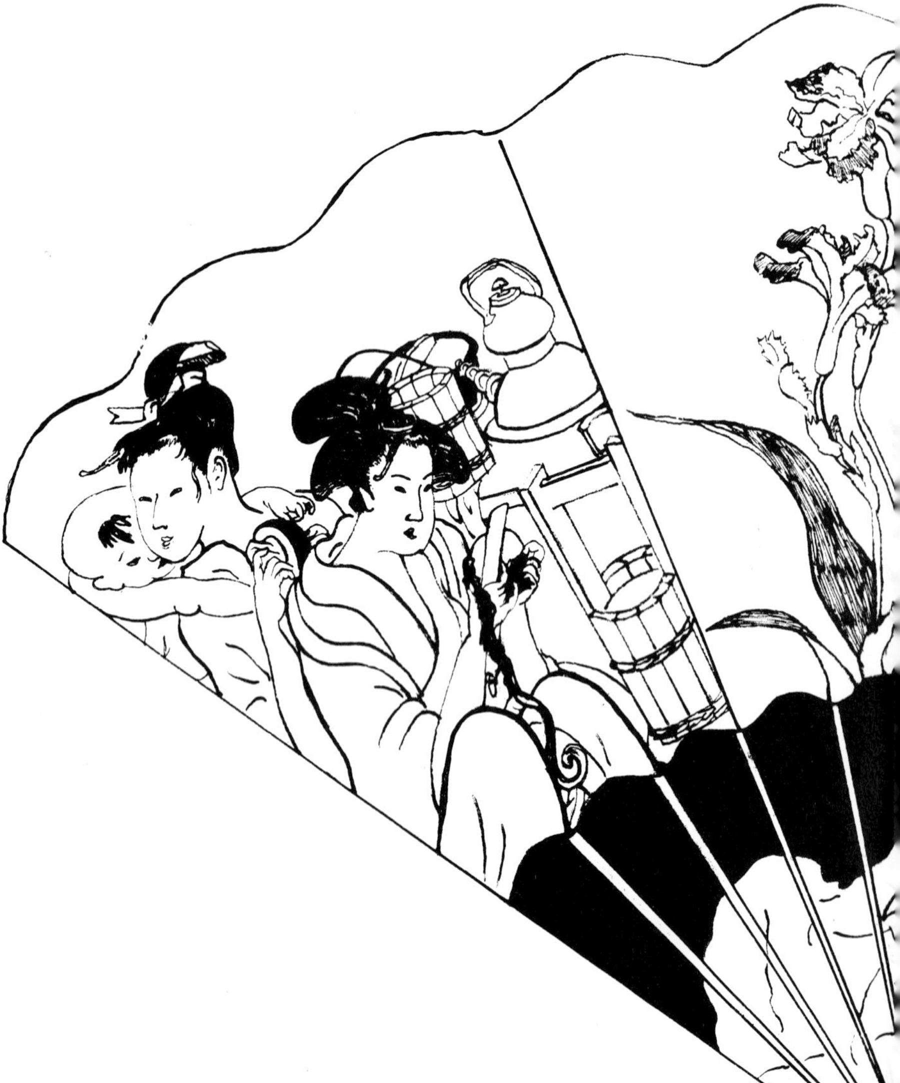

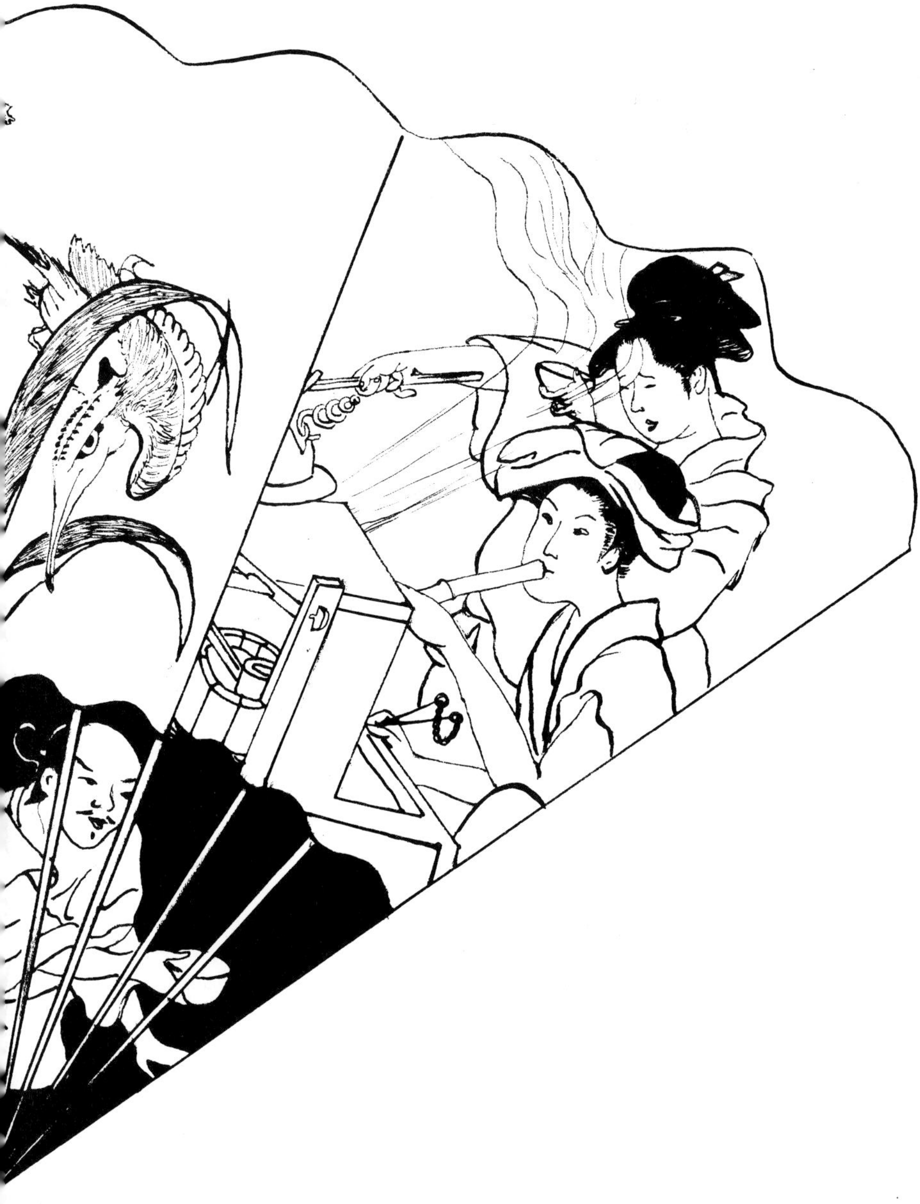

# TWO TIMES TWO IN DOMESTIC INTERIOR

I
One peels vegetables
letting the curling peels
drop into her lap.

The other,
drying a lacquered bowl,
cares for the child on her back,
whose forelock rises like a brush
on his shaven skull.

On the stove stand an iron kettle
and a covered dish.
The water-bucket beside it
is made of varnished wood
and tied with ropes of braided rush.

Tortoise-shell combs and pins
pull back the women's hair
and hold it in place.

There is little room to move
inside this 'floating world'.
No window opens on trees,
no screen gives shelter
from the sun.
There are neither depth,
nor shadows.
The scene is so clear, you can see
the grain in the wood,
the threads in the cotton jackets.

II
One crouches before the fire,
blows through a bamboo pipe
to kindle the flames.

The other, ladling tea
into her cup,
holds up her left arm to her face
and closes her eyes
against the smoke.

III
In the garden
two men use indigo
to print irises and kingfishers
on a piece of silk
stretched between two poles.

A troupe of traveling musicians
goes past.
Two acrobats wearing demon masks
casually walk beside them
on their hands.

It is rumoured that the man
who made these woodcuts
is on the run
from the emperor's secret police.

He broke the law
against portraying the life
of the lower class.

But the two women know
his whereabouts:
this moment he is sitting
cross-legged on the porch of their house,
waiting for his bowl of rice
and fried cormorant.

# EPILOGUE

He has waited in the wings
too long. Too often
he was jostled back into the corridors
by the changing crowds,
the hero in frills and daggers,
the lady's fawning entourage.

He found himself backstage
with half a heart,
a single glove,
a one-armed juggler,
a cast without script,
a curtain and no call.

He was an extra's extra.
Someone else spoke the dialogue,
set the stage,
heard the prompter's whisper,
collected the earnings;
his cue never came.

In crowd scenes he was second
from the left in the last row.
Once he picked up a ribbon,
once he sneezed,
once he stumbled over a shoe.
One time the director moved him
from left to right.

He was less noticed than the props,
the rickety table, the painted
backdrop, the piece of rug.

But tonight he has taken over,
selected the scenery,
stepped into the centre
till curtain fall.

It is dark, rainy and cold.
He is sitting inside the railings
at the edge of the canal.

He is wearing his heavy black coat.
One pocket contains his role book,
all lines crossed out
except for the final directions:

Exit. Fade to blackout.

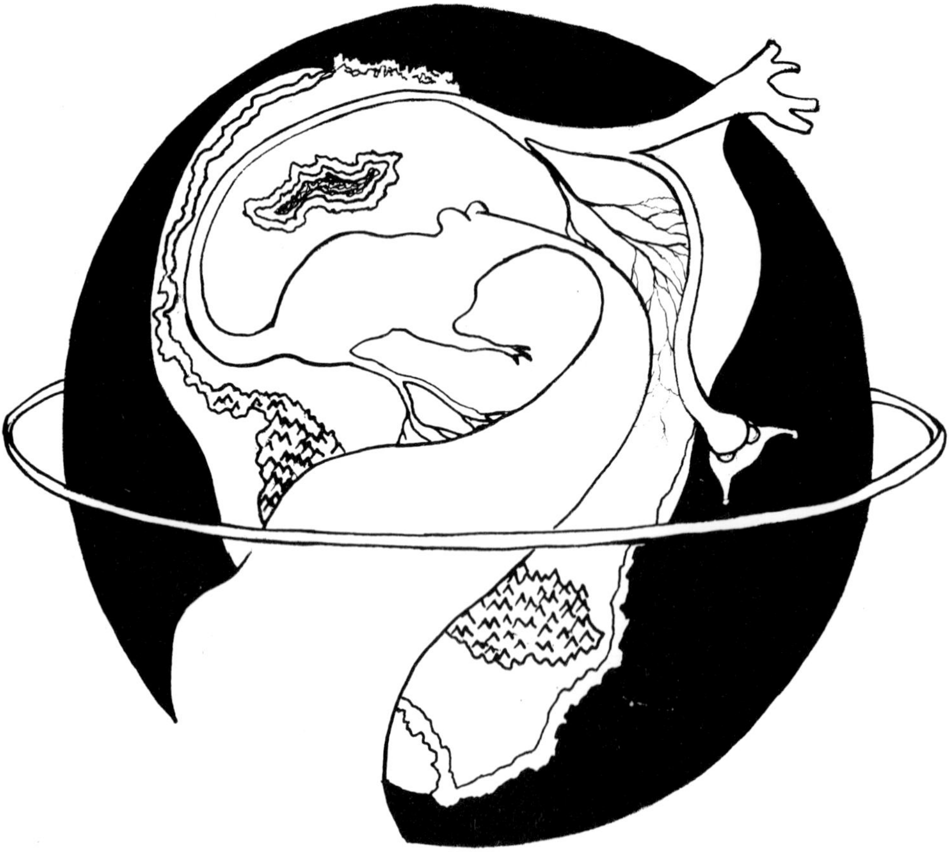

## A RAT'S TALE

When I was a young and nosy rat,
I found on a beach
between rubbish and splinters
of glass and bones
a sleeping heart
which had gone astray,
and slipping in
to warm myself,
I put my ear to the wall
of a ventricle,
not far from the aorta,
to listen to the grass growing.

On closer inspection
I found that it was a continent
full of white areas
that would have taken more
than a lifetime to explore;
there were polar regions
too cold even for the feet
of a penguin.
A red-hot ring went around it,
a blue lake had danger notices
on its banks,
two great streams
transported animals,
blind molluscs, flatheaded toads,
luminous fish.
From deep forests rose
the sound of drumming
and on high plains stood
ghost towns
and abandoned temples
of sullen gods.

As I traveled from ventricle
to ventricle,
I found in the suburbs of a city
a small dark house
where at a table somebody sat,
listening to something
like an endless pounding.

This heart was lying there,
the limp bellows
of a grinding organ.
I felt sorry for it
and its unused possibilites
and its useless past.
I brought it home
for my small brood.
It nourished a whole family
for a while,
that good heart.

## WHERE HAS THE DRAPER GONE?

A pink house, a black door,
a white name on black ground:
Margaret Joyce.

A drapershop window,
a lace curtain, a rainpipe,
a little man in black.

The colour of the house
is pale cerise,
party-dress pink.

The colour of the jetcoal door
is mourning crepe,
but the dark shadow behind it
is funeral suit shade, a shade
blacker than black.

The draper doesn't seem to be there.

She was here,
it is written over the shop,
proof enough.

The coordinates of the window frame
are still dissecting
her pale blue cardigan
hanging empty and limp
from a hanger
that's hung from the border
of a snowy lace curtain
in the window.

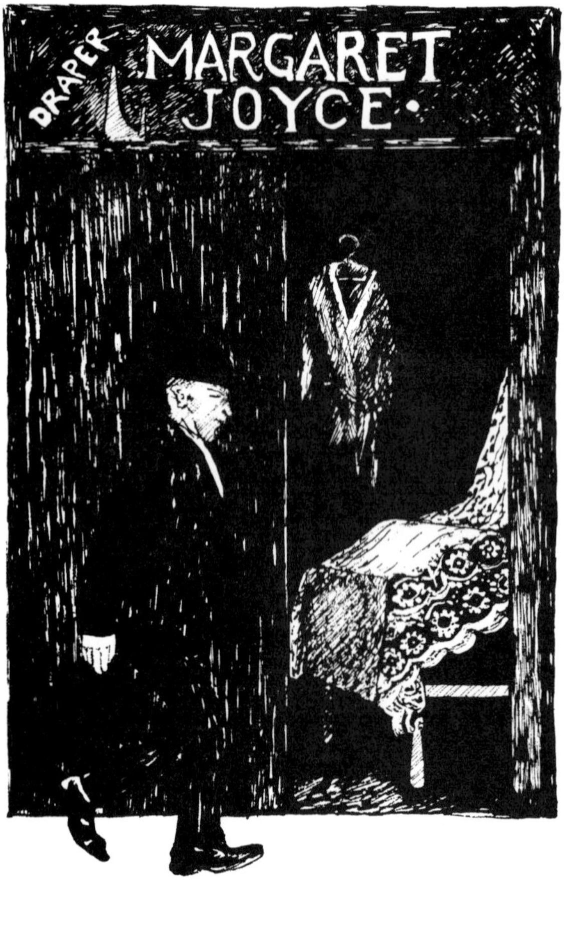
DRAPER
MARGARET
JOYCE

But inside no soul in sight.

Did she go off with black bag, hat,
down the road, smiling
saying hello to neighbours?
Popular Mrs. Joyce.
But why did she leave the door half open?
So unlike her.
Why is white lace draping
a table inside?
A flash of lace in the dark.
Is it a bridal dress?
Is it the bride on the table,
laid out in her organdy and tulle?

Why won't the little man in black
who is hurrying his polished boots
towards the black door
in the pink house tell

where the draper has gone?

## AFTER DEPORTATION

The houses bend
around the corner
as if they were planning
shady deals.

The streets are one single
curfew.

The ground shrinks
from under the feet,
as lips pull back from teeth
in pain.

The doors turn their backs,
not one of the entrances
leads into the open.

The stairs writhe
and moan.

Rid of their occupants,
the rooms scurry together
and give witness of nothing

except a handful of velvet in a corner,
trampled carpet-flowers
bled to dust.

The floor is scarred
where the table stood.

Brass flickers from the window-handle,

shatters
the contour of a face
in the mirror,

breaks the light sharply
and finally.

The windows crack with screams.

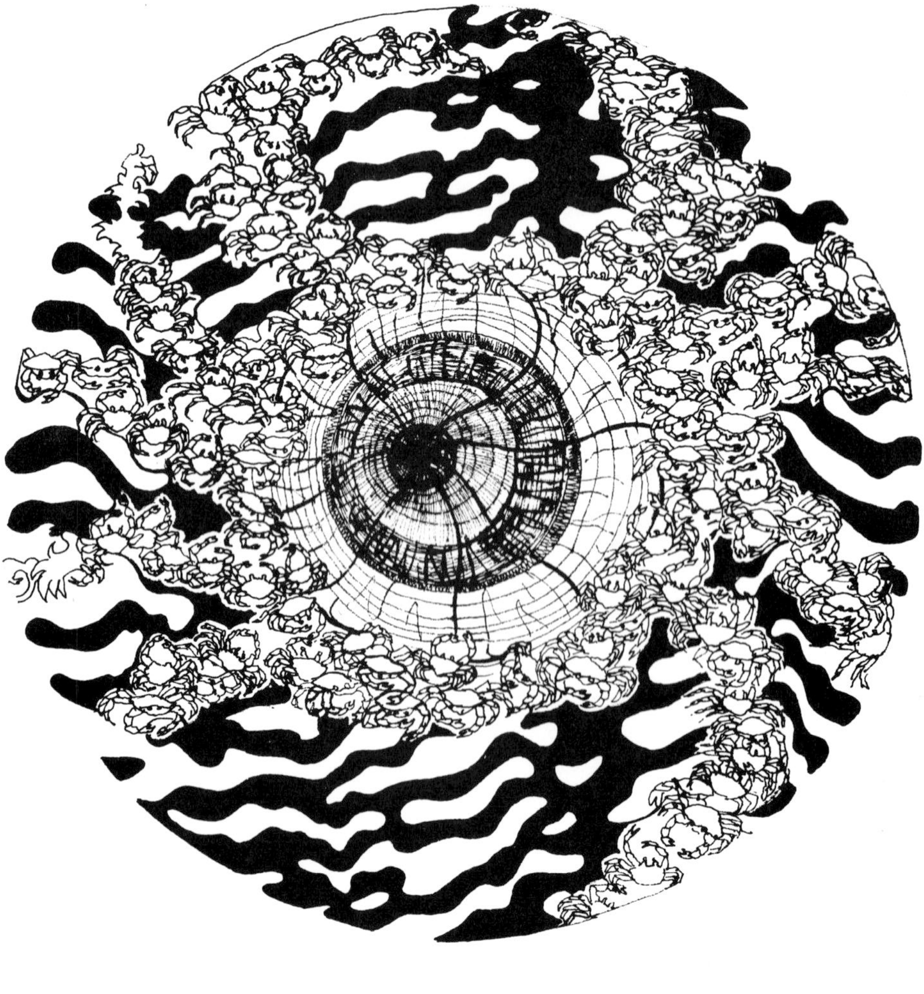

# THE LORDS OF THE ISLAND

Out of the water
before the coast of one
of the two Americas
grows the sharp-curved claw
of an island,
the fang perhaps
of a drowned fire-spewing dragon.

Its dark volcanic mouth
gapes wide open
on the bottom of a fresh-water lake,
enclosed by the stony ring
of a reef.
The crater is still brimful
with murky caustic sediments.
The air-sailing birds
know the lake's malignant navel well
and keep their distance.
From above it is a funnel, bubbling
with inorganic poisons,
the crystal-violet focus
of the concentric circles
of lake, reef and sea.

All round here
live the sideways moving crabs.
Once there were only few,
now they multiply rapidly,
nineteen to the dozen.
They are the birds' spiteful enemies.
With their claws they fish
tiny nestlings
out of nests built cleverly
into crevices between the rocks.

Carrion draws them.
They crawl singlemindedly,
moving in their millions
on dead and decomposing matter.
They glut the reef.
Lacking space on the strand,
a pink swell when the moon is out,
they clamber over each other,
rubbing and grinding shell
upon shell,
with sightless and stalked eyes,
a troop of armoured killers
from some bygone war,
but ready for action.

There was a village here.
While trying to rescue
the survivors of a shipwreck
all the men were killed
except for the lighthouse keeper.
A few women and children were left.
They ate coconuts and fish.

Then the watchman forced the women
one by one into his tower
and raped them,
until one slew him.

Weeks later a boat arrived
and brought them away.

Since then no-one
disputes the crabs' dominion
over the island.

## THE MADMAN AND THE TREE

The tree is passé –
so they say,
maybe rightly so;
it has certainly ceased
to serve as proof
of anything beyond its own existence.

The madman, however,
despite speedy atomic overheads,
minds the sky for clouds alone;
his thoughts turn on
withering bud,
wrinkled leaf and creased fruit.

His favourite toy
the perpetuum mobile
of rising sap
and falling branch.
He gets drunk on chlorophyll.

The brown of the bark
is his darling, his flower
of meta-language.

Light, I need light
and unmelting molecules, he cries,
see that the tree is the tree,
let it be
the deep green of the avocado pear
on a background of lilac
(causing all tree-surgeons
to recoil with horror and all art lovers
to sob with joy),
or in high summer
bony and wind-shorn
in its peculiar brightness of soil.

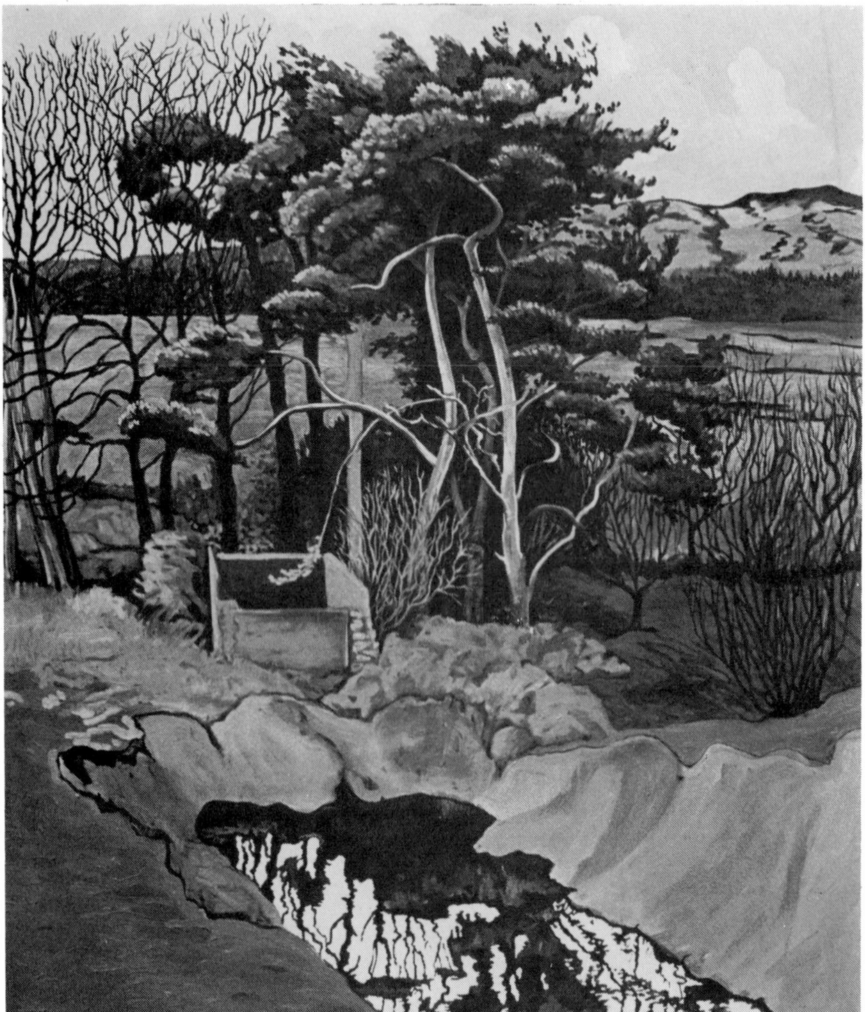

All points of the compass
serve him
to make the tree –
inside out
and upside down,
oil-, chalk- and wax-trees,
arboreous crystals,
celestial trees,
fathers of the Trojan horse,
walled-in and dismantled,
and busy with photosynthesis,
the cleverest of all its sylvan tricks.

Now that the end
of all this annoying tree-talk
is near,
the need for it is growing
subversively:
it seems that in secret meeting-places
increasing numbers of lunatics
are whispering together
about trees about trees

## THIRTEEN WAYS OF LOOKING AT A ROCKET
(adapted from Wallace Stevens)

I
Among twenty green hills
the only moving thing
the blinking metal of a rocket.

II
I was of three minds
like a rocket
in which there are three warheads.

III
The rocket whizzed past in the autumn winds.
It was a small part of the pantomime.

IV
A man and a woman
are one.
A man and a woman and a rocket
are nothing.

V
I do not know which frightens me more,
the deadliness of Trident 2
the flexibility of the Cruise Missile
the rocket exploding
or just after.

VI
Radioactive dust filled the long window
with barbaric clouds,
the shadow of the rocket
crossed it, to and fro.
The mood traced in the shadow
a decipherable end.

VII
O old men of the Pentagon,
why do you imagine anti-missile missiles?

Do you not see how the rocket
dematerializes the feet
of the women about you?

## VIII
I know killer-accents
and threatening, inescapable rhythms.
but I know, too,
that the rocket is involved
in what I know.

## IX
When the rocket flew out of sight,
it marked the edge
of one of many circles.

## X
At the sight of rockets
flying in a grey light,
even the warning cries of the physicists
will be silenced.

## XI
He rode over the Atlantic
in an armoured plane.
Once, a fear pierced him,
in that he mistook
the shadow of his aircraft
for rockets.

## XII
The river is standing still.
The rocket must be flying.

## XIII
It was night all day.
It was raining dust
and it was going to rain dust.
The rocket sat
on a dead earth.